JELLY BEANS

*****

JOSEPH MCNAIR STOVER

*one act original scenes for
two, three and four players*

DRAMATIC LINES, TWICKENHAM, ENGLAND

text copyright © Joseph McNair Stover

This book is intended to provide resource material for speech and drama festivals, workshops, examinations and for use in schools and colleges.

Application for performance by professional companies should be made to:

Dramatic Lines
PO Box 201
Twickenham
TW2 5RQ
England

A CIP record for this book is available from the British Library

ISBN 0 9522224 7 7

Jelly Beans first published
1998
by
Dramatic Lines Twickenham England

Printed by The Dramatic Lines Press
Twickenham England

for Amanda

CONTENTS

THE ELEVATOR

Cast:	3 female
Playing Time:	10 minutes
Costumes:	Contemporary dress
Properties:	2 shopping bags/hold-alls, bag jelly beans, tap shoes, cribbage game, lighter, candles, nail file
Setting:	An elevator
Lighting:	No special effects
Characters:	Donna
	Sarah
	Joane

DONNA and SARAH strangers to one another,
get on an elevator in a high-rise building,
each with a bag

DONNA: Ninety-four, please.

SARAH: *(Pushes button, then another.)* And ninety-nine for me.

DONNA: *(After a few moments of silence.)* Oh, look at this!
(Exasperated. Points above elevator doors.)
This is the slow elevator. It will take forever to get to the
ninety-fourth floor.

SARAH: Yes, we should have waited for one of the others.

DONNA: This is a fairly new building, you know. It's supposed
to have all the up-to-date features. And here we are,
plugging along at the speed of one of the first models.

1

SARAH: I know what you mean. It's probably as unsafe
            as one of the first ones, too. Cables breaking .....
            *(Stops herself. Together they turn their eyes
            toward the ceiling, then to the floor.)*

DONNA: No. It's much safer. I know because I don't like elevators
            and so I asked the manager. They're all equipped with
            special brakes if the cable should ... separate.

SARAH: *(Confidentially.)* I don't like elevators either.
            But my doctor .... *(She shrugs.)*

DONNA: Oh, he's in here? My sister's insurance company, too.
            Ninety-fourth floor. Nobody needs to have an office
            in the clouds. It's ridiculous.

SARAH: I agree. *(Pause.)* Of course, there's nothing to guarantee
            against getting stuck between floors.

DONNA: *(Taken aback.)* **What?**

SARAH: Well, I don't mean to alarm you, but if the power goes off
            we could get stuck. Like that time in New York when they had
            that city-wide power failure.

DONNA: Oh dear!

SARAH: People were stuck for hours.

DONNA: Oh! *(Fretfully.)* Oh, no! Oh, no!

SARAH: Now, now! We must stay calm. *(DONNA gasps,
            holds her breath.)* What is it?

DONNA: *(Softly.)* I thought I heard something.
            (Together they listen.) No, nothing.

SARAH: Don't scare me like that.

DONNA: Scare **you**? You're the one
            who brought up power failures.

SARAH: Look, I simply feel there's nothing wrong
            with being prepared.

DONNA: How can we prepare when we're already on our way?
           We have no tools, nothing.

SARAH: *(Considers.)* You're right. But wait. Let's take stock of what
           we **do** have. All right?

DONNA: Okay.

SARAH: *(Looks in bag.)* First priority ..... food. *(Holds jelly beans aloft.)*
           Jelly beans! We can each have half. If we space them properly
           we can do quite well. How about you?

DONNA: Sorry, nothing.

SARAH: Okay. Next: something to keep us occupied. Fortunately I'm seeing
           my doctor today. And you know how long a wait **that** can be.
           I have a cribbage board and cards.

DONNA: Marvelous! I know how to play. We could have a tournament.

SARAH: Now, don't get carried away ... Uh? ...Uh?

DONNA: Donna.

SARAH: Sarah. Remember, we're not looking **forward**
           to something happening.

DONNA: I know. But it was getting so exciting. I **love** jelly beans.

SARAH: Okay. Now, there's an emergency phone in here
           but we can't count on that working.
           We'll need a way to communicate with rescuers.

DONNA: *(Thoughtfully.)* I can scream fairly well.

SARAH: Pardon?

DONNA: Whenever we have school plays and they need a scream
           to come from off stage, I do it.
           I can reach some pretty high notes. Want to listen?
           (Takes a deep breath in preparation for demonstration.)

SARAH: *(Quickly.)* No, no. That's okay. Besides, I was,
           I was hoping for something a little more useful.

DONNA: Are you sure? I have a range of six octaves.
I could sound exactly like a ninety-nine year-old man
getting squashed by a ten ton truck .....
(Looks at SARAH's *stern face.)* I suppose not.

SARAH: No. We don't want them to think there's a murder taking place
on the elevator. *(Logically.)* How embarrassing do you think
that would look if they got the doors opened and one of us
wasn't dead?

DONNA: I guess they'd be a little disappointed.

SARA: Not only that, we might get written up in the newspapers
as a couple of lunatics.

DONNA: You're right. I wouldn't want anybody to think we were crazy.

SARAH: Okay. So screaming is out. What else can we do?
My father was in the navy and I learned Morse code from him.
But what have we got to tap it out with?

DONNA: Tap! I'm taking tap dancing lessons and I've got my tap shoes
with me. You could tell me the code, and I can tap on the floor.
Do you think you could tell me how to ask for help to the tune of
'Tea for Two'? *(Starts to dance a little, not very well.)*

SARAH: *(Skeptically.)* How long have you been taking lessons?

DONNA: Well, my problem is I don't get to practise very much.
My father says I sound like a flock of woodpeckers
destroying our house, so I can't do it around him.
And during the day I'm busy with more important matters. Such as
my tuba lessons. Oh! If only I had my tuba with me
I could blow out Morse code. I'm much better at that
than I am with tap dancing.

SARAH: Uh ... let's forget about the idea of trying to communicate with anybody
for the moment. Okay? Let's consider what else we might need.

DONNA: All right.

SARAH: Mmm. *(To herself.)* What's next then?

DONNA: Oh! If the power goes off, so will the lights. We won't be able to see!

SARAH: Say, that would be a problem. In fact, I can't think of anything worse than waiting for help in the dark.

DONNA: Or playing cribbage in the dark.

SARAH: Hold on, I have a lighter in my bag. Bergy's birthday present.
Bergy's my friend. He doesn't smoke but I'm trying to get him started.
(DONNA looks confused. SARAH sees her expression.)
I like the smell of tobacco, you see?
(DONNA nods slowly, uncertain.) Uh-huh! If we keep the flame going it'll run out of fuel in no time.

DONNA: *(Brightens.)* Candles! I bought candles for my sister's dinner party tonight. Oh, yeah! **I have the candles!**
(Starts bouncing up and down on her toes.)

SARAH: *(Caught up in DONNA's enthusiasm.)* Then we're all set!
We'll survive! We'll survive!
(Both join in a happy embrace, eyes closed tightly.
The third person, JOANE, comes on stage and enters elevator.
She stops, startled, when she sees DONNA and SARAH.
Carefully she goes around and stands behind them.)

JOANE: One hundred, please. *(DONNA and SARAH, still clutching each other, open their eyes wide and stare at audience.)*

DONNA: What was that?

JOANE: One hundred. *(DONNA and SARAH separate and turn their heads.)*

SARAH: Where...?

DONNA: Well, **you** have a lot of nerve.

JOANE: I beg your pardon?

SARAH: Now, now. *(Takes DONNA's arm, leads her aside.)*
It's not entirely her fault.

DONNA: But she's ruining everything.
How can we play cribbage with three people?

SARAH: Don't worry. We can work something out. Take turns.

DONNA: *(Upset.)* That will leave one person with nothing to do, while the other two have fun. I don't like that.
(Suddenly thinks of something.)
Jelly beans! *(Whispers.)* Now we'll have to share them.

SARAH: You've got a point there. *(Looks at JOANE. JOANE and SARAH smile politely at each other. To DONNA.)*
We'll have to get her to leave. Immediately.

DONNA: I've got an idea. *(Turns to JOANE. Smiles. Looks away. Smiles at JOANE again, looks away. Clears her throat.)*
I understand this building has a **very** lovely stairwell.

JOANE: *(Not interested.)* Oh?

DONNA: Yes. Quite lovely. It has ... well, of course, stairs ...
a nice iron railing ..... cute NO SMOKING signs ....
(Trails off. Turns back to SARAH.) Forget it.

SARAH: *(Whispers.)* We may have to use force.

DONNA: **What?!**

SARAH. It's our only chance. I could hit the button for the upcoming floor. We stop. And you shove her out.

DONNA: Me? Why me?

SARAH: You look more intimidating.

DONNA: *(Insulted.)* Well, I don't know if I like that.

SARAH: You want to live through this ordeal or not?

DONNA: *(Uncertain. Sighs.)* Oh, all right.

SARAH: Look, if it will make you feel any better, I'll help you nudge her closer to the door so it will be easier.

DONNA: Thank you. *(Together they turn. Side by side, backs to the audience, they take a step forward. Another step. Another. Finally they are directly in front of JOANE, their shoulders and heads framing JOANE's head. She is filing her nails, unconcerned. She looks up past them.)*

JOANE: Whose floor?

DONNA: What?

JOANE: Whose floor? *(DONNA and SARAH turn around.)*

DONNA: Oh ... it's ... it's uh! ... mine. *(Giggles.)*
           It's **mine,** Sarah. I made it.

SARAH: Yeah. *(Shrugs.)*

DONNA: *(Embarrassed.)* Bye. *(She exits.)*

SARAH: *(Alone with JOANE. Long pause. SARAH turns to JOANE.)*
           Have you ever considered the safety of elevators?

TRIPLE PLAY

Cast:	1 male, 1 female
Playing time:	10 minutes
Costumes:	Contemporary dress
Properties:	None
Setting:	An urban sidewalk
Lighting:	No special effects
Characters:	Nancy
	Doug

NANCY and DOUG approach each other
from opposite sides of the stage.
They notice each other. Stop and speak.

DOUG: You look very familiar.

NANCY: So do you.

DOUG: Nancy?

NANCY: Doug?

DOUG }
NANCY}   Yes!! *(Both become awkward and shy.)*

DOUG: Well. You look different. But 1 recognized you.

NANCY: Yeah. You've changed some ..... Long time since .....
           You ... you going steady?

DOUG: No. You?

8

NANCY: *(Shakes head.)* Nuh.

DOUG: Really? I felt sure ...... Well! Who can ever predict? Right?

NANCY: *(Pause.)* You think our personalities have changed much?
           I mean, we're more mature now. At least, I would hope.
           We wouldn't have those dumb teenage fights we were always starting.
           Don't you agree?

DOUG: *(Shrugs.)* I don't know. Maybe. *(Thoughtfully.)* Wouldn't that
           be funny? To run into each other after all this time and find out
           we've become ..... *(Meaningfully.)* compatible?
           (Very long pause with both of them fidgeting and eyeing one another.)
           .... But then again, ... *(Lightly.)* we might be even worse with each
           other.

NANCY: *(Laughs. Then considers what he's said.)* Actually, if you and I
           really stop to think about it, there **were** some rather basic differences
           between us that probably even time wouldn't have changed.
           (Relaxes a little.) So I guess we don't have to be awkward
           with each other, right? I mean, if there's no hope of us really getting
           back together, we don't have to be shy and watch what we say.

DOUG: *(Smiles.)* Yeah. *(Pause.)* **Whew!** That was strange, too.
           I was thinking there for a moment, 'Have Nancy and I got a
           chance to make up and start dating again after all this time.'
           My heart was pounding.

NANCY: Mine too. All the memories of the good times
           replayed through my head. I felt as though I'd stepped into a dream,
           with my old dream-date standing there right in front of me
           ready to make good on missed opportunities.

DOUG: *(Agrees earnestly.)* Yes! Yes! Exactly.
           But ... you're right. We have some basic, and major,
           differences between us. It would never have worked out ......
           then or now.

NANCY.   *(Throws out her arms.)* Like a weight off my shoulders! I feel
           I can act natural now and just sit down and talk with you.
           Find out what you've been doing. What have you been doing?

DOUG: College. Studied computer science. I design video games now.

NANCY: Really? Well, I'm still after what I said I was going after all
             this time: marine biology. I'm working on a doctorate.

DOUG: Great. That's great.

NANCY: So, how are the wonderful Mr. and Mrs. Bennet getting along?

DOUG: Who?

NANCY: Your parents. I certainly don't mean your **great** grand-parents.

DOUG: *(Blankly.)* Bennet? My parents' last name isn't Bennet.

NANCY: *(Stares at him.)* But then, how could you be Doug Bennet?

DOUG: I'm not. *(Pause.)* Aren't you Nancy Holder?

NANCY: Not nearly. Nothing like.

DOUG: Oh my.

NANCY: 'Oh my', is right. *(Pause. Uncomfortably.)* Now we're back to
             awkward again. I don't know you ..... you don't know me.

DOUG: *(Embarrassed.)* I know. I know.

NANCY: I .. I .... feel awfully silly.

DOUG: You're not alone. *(Pause. Looks at her.)* I guess we could decide
             now if we **want** to know each other.

NANCY: *(Nods. Silence. Impulsively.)* Do you have someplace you have to go?
             Somebody to meet? *(DOUG shakes his head.)* Neither do I.

DOUG: Well ..... *(Thinks.)* Maybe this is a sign.
             How likely is it that a Doug and a Nancy would bump into each other,
             think they were old steadys, and find out they were wrong?

NANCY: It's incredible. And it wouldn't have happened
             if we hadn't **looked** familiar, you know? *(Stands back and
             appraises him. Lightly.)* You don't look **too** bad at that.

DOUG: *(Smiles.)* Well, that's a good start, seeing as how you don't look
             too chewed up yourself.

NANCY: *(Laughs.)* Thanks. Shall we exchange background
           information? *(DOUG nods agreeably.)* I'll go first then:
           I had a fairly happy childhood, although I ought to mention that
           I was raised by dolphins off the coast of Florida
           after my parents' yacht sank and I was set adrift
           in my crib. I tend to think that this experience
           triggered my interest in marine biology.

DOUG: *(Strokes chin.)* Hmmm. A good sense of humor.

NANCY: Uh! **Oh!** Am I going to have to pass some sort of check-list?

DOUG: I wouldn't call it **that**. Let's just say there are one or two qualities
           I look for in a female. If they're not there, then looks, wealth and
           status are all academic. They're **nice**, but I'm old-fashioned.
           I like to talk to a woman more than show her off.

NANCY: I wouldn't call that old-fashioned. Sounds like you've got it
           reversed. I'd say you were refreshingly progressive.
           Some men still resent women's suffrage.

DOUG: Ah, yes. The pedestal theory. All objects set atop it considered
           fragile. I keep a block of cement on top of mine.

NANCY: I see you have a sense of humor, too.

DOUG: Is that important?

NANCY: **Very.**

DOUG: You have your own check-list, I see.
           Well! I guess it's my turn to talk about my childhood. I must confess
           that I didn't have the privilege of being brought up by dolphins ....
           Wombats, in my case. Marsupials, you know. Had a heck of a time
           getting in and out of Mom's pouch. Especially after the age of five.
           Poor Mom. I left her at the airport in Australia with tears in her eyes.
           I would have brought her along, Dad too, but they would have had to
           stay in quarantine six months.

NANCY: *(Mock-serious.)* You're not making this up?

DOUG: How could I make up a story like that?

NANCY: *(Playfully.)* Hmm. I'm not sure my adopted parents would approve of my dating anyone with your history. You're simply not **aquatic** enough.

DOUG: Not aquatic? What about the floods of '87 when my whole family had to swim for their lives?

NANCY: I'm not sure that counts.

DOUG: Well ... my parents might raise objections or a similar nature. Can your family climb trees?

NANCY: Certainly not. Wouldn't be dignified.

DOUG: What's dignity got to do with it?

NANCY: Can you imagine what people would say if they saw my mother or father up a Florida palm? There'd be a scandal! Everyone would think they were lunatics.

DOUG: **Lunatics!** Are you suggesting something about my folks?

NANCY: I'm simply pointing out the consequences of such actions.

DOUG: Well, in Australia they'd make '*Wombat Digest*', front page. They'd be looked up to.

NANCY: I imagine so, being in trees.

DOUG: *(Groans.)* Poor. Very poor.

NANCY: *(Laughs.)* Now that we've gotten our backgrounds out of the way, shall we get together sometime, despite our parents?

DOUG: By all means. Free tonight?

NANCY: Yes.

DOUG: Terrific. Call you?

NANCY: Uh-huh! I'll write down my phone number .... Oh! we're forgetting something. *(Sticks out hand.)* I'm Nancy Brock.

DOUG: Doug Fine. *(They look at each other.)*

NANCY: The Doug Fine who stapled my ponytail to the bulletin board?

DOUG: The Nancy Brock who retaliated by slashing my bicycle
               tires with a pair of scissors?

NANCY: I **should** have done worse.

DOUG: You **couldn't** have done worse. I had to push my bike home
               in the worst rain of the century. A car went by
               and splashed mud on me head to foot.

NANCY: Good.

DOUG: Good? Was what I did so terrible?

NANCY: I had to stand there through lunch until Cindy Trent
               came looking for me. And I had a crick in my neck
               from having to stare at the ceiling.

DOUG: You can't expect me to believe you couldn't have gotten
               yourself free on your own.

NANCY: I **couldn't!**

DOUG: Afraid of losing a strand or two of that precious hair you washed
               and fluffed three times a night?

NANCY: There's nothing wrong with a person wanting to keep
               up their appearance. I was proud of my nice hair.

DOUG: Looks as though you still are.

NANCY: Well, it's apparent that vanity is no where **near** your problem.

DOUG: What is that supposed to mean? You calling me a slob?

NANCY: You're certainly no Handsome Harry.

DOUG: You said, only a short while ago, that I wasn't bad looking.

NANCY: What I said was you weren't **too** bad looking.

DOUG: I can see time hasn't changed you much.

NANCY: You either. Excuse me, I'm late.

DOUG: Thought you said you didn't have anywhere to go just now.

NANCY: I just remembered I have an appointment.

DOUG: With your hair dresser?
             I'd chip in a few bucks if I thought It'd do any good.

        (NANCY stalks away. Stops, turns, sticks out her tongue. Walks off.
        DOUG stands looking after her. Pause. Sticks out his tongue.
        DOUG exits.)

THE MIRROR

Cast:	2 female
Playing time:	10 minutes
Costumes:	Contemporary dress
Properties:	None
Setting:	Two bedrooms separated by two dressing tables set back to back (that share a framed mirror)
Lighting:	No special effects
Characters:	Linda
	Joyce

LINDA and JOYCE are at the dressing table in their bedroom.

LINDA:}
JOYCE:}   Nothing ever exciting happens to me.

(Both go to mirror to contemplate image.)

LINDA: *(Surprised.)* Boy, I look terrible.

JOYCE: You're telling me.

LINDA: Hey!

JOYCE: Hey!

(Each puts a hand to the mirror. They rotate their hands, one against the other, synchronized. as though touching the mirror.)

LINDA: You're not me.

JOYCE:	Thank goodness for that.
LINDA:	Well, get out of my mirror!
JOYCE:	I'm not in anything, except my bedroom. You're the one who's stuck in the mirror. *(Pause.)* Isn't it cramped?
LINDA:	Very funny. Listen. I've got a date tonight, and even though it's with boring old Arnold I want to look good. So get lost and send me, or whoever it is that's supposed to be in there, back.
JOYCE:	This is out of my hands. Honest. It's never happened before. Are you sure you're not a piece of glass?
LINDA:	Don't get insulting. *(Pause.)* Hmmm. This is kind of interesting you know?
JOYCE:	*(Aside.)* Not from my perspective.
LINDA:	I bet I know what's going on. You're my alter ego, sent here to help me learn about myself. Yeah, that's it. Turn around.
JOYCE:	What?
LINDA:	Turn around. I want to see what my other side looks like. *(JOYCE shrugs and turns around slowly.)*
LINDA:	Boy, am I in bad shape.
JOYCE:	*(Indignant.)* Hey!
LINDA:	No offense. But I ... you, could lose a few pounds.
JOYCE:	How would you like to lose a few teeth?
LINDA:	Try it. How can you reach me?

JOYCE: *(Puts both hands against the mirror but can't push through.)*
You're right. So, what are we going to do?
Just stand here and criticize each other?

LINDA: No. that would be a waste of a valuable opportunity.
This thing ..... whatever it is that's going on,
might not last very long. We should make good use of the time.

JOYCE: *(To herself.)* Maybe if I went back to bed and got up tomorrow .....

ILINDA: Are you listening to me?

JOYCE: Yes, yes. But I don't see much good coming of this.

LINDA: Don't you?
By exploring our opposites we can get to know ourselves better.

JOYCE: Who cares?

LINDA: Well. I'm already learning something.

JOYCE: *(Suspiciously.)* Like what?

LINDA: Like, I'm inquisitive and you're not.
Say, are you going on a date tonight, too?

JOYCE: Forget it. I'd rather go horseback riding.

LINDA: You're kidding.

JOYCE: No. A Horse doesn't talk back. If you don't want to see him
you don't have to, without having to make an excuse for his benefit.
And when you're tired of him, you just send him home.

LINDA: *(Considers this.)* That's true.
(Pause.) But then again, I don't have to worry about Arnold
kicking me in the head. And I don't have to feed him every day.
(Smiles.) He feeds me. I also don't have to buy him new shoes.
Then there's the fact that .....

JOYCE: *(Brusquely.)* Okay. Okay. We both have reasons
for keeping the company we do. So what?

LINDA: *(Shrugs, a little hurt. Tentatively.)* Do you like to go dancing?

JOYCE: No. Bowling.

LINDA: Do you like long dresses?

JOYCE: Jeans.

LINDA: Chopin?

JOYCE: The Plastic Slugs.

LINDA: *(Sighs.)* Favourite Color?

JOYCE: *(Bored.)* Blue.

LINDA: What? Blue? But that's mine, too.
                Hunh. So that means that even though we're different,
                we're not exact opposites. *(Nods.)* Interesting.

JOYCE: *(Throws up her hands. Mocking.)* Interesting. Interesting.

LINDA: Well, it is. You obviously have very little patience.

JOYCE: I can summon it up from the depths of my 'horsy' personality
                if I need to.
LINDA: So can't you try using a little bit now?
                Let's try to keep going. Please?

JOYCE: *(Pause. Grudgingly.)* Okay.

LINDA: Terrific! Favorite season?

JOYCE: Spring.

LINDA: Mine, too! Favorite flower?

JOYCE: Tulip.

LINDA: Yes! Favorite time of day?

JOYCE: *(Getting interested.)* Morning.

LINDA: Favorite smell?

JOYCE: *(Excited.)* Bread baking.

LINDA: This is wonderful!
                Favorite sound?

JOYCE: Birds singing.

LINDA: *(Closes her eyes and spreads out her arms, caught up in the moment.)*
                Favorite food?

JOYCE: *(Hugging herself.)* Stewed tomatoes!

                (LINDA gasps. Holds stomach. Makes gagging sounds.)

JOYCE: *(Archly.)* You have a problem with stewed tomatoes?

LINDA: I'm sorry. I was just expecting something more along the lines of
                ice cream ..... cake .....

JOYCE: *(Expressively.)* Boiled with plenty of jalapeno peppers!
                (Explains.) I like my stewed tomatoes sitting up and winking at me.

                (LINDA stares, mouth agape.)

JOYCE: *(With satisfied smile over* LINDA's *reaction.)*
                My horse enjoys a bowl now and again, too.

LINDA: *(Shrugs. Clears throat.)* Yes, well ..... I guess the list
                had to end somewhere.

JOYCE: I suppose.

LINDA: You know, we're actually getting along better than I thought we would.
                We're compatible because of our very differences.
                Am I making sense? *(JOYCE shakes head no.)*
                There are places missing in us. Like a gear, with teeth.
                There are empty slots which only a complimentary gear can fill.
                Now do you get it?

JOYCE: Sort of. *(Warms to the idea.)* Like a horse is one thing,
                and a person is another,but together they make something new.

LINDA: *(To herself.)* Horses again. *(To JOYCE.)* Yeah, something like that.

JOYCE: Um, I'm sorry if I snapped at you earlier.
This has been kind of fun.

LINDA: Oh, that's okay. I think this whole mirror deal sort of threw us.

JOYCE: Yeah. The mirror. I forgot you're not really here,
over here with me. *(Shrugs. Grudgingly.)* I almost wish you could be.
Over here, that is.

LINDA: *(Laughs lightly.)* No. No, it would never work out.

JOYCE: *(Surprised.)* What do you mean? You've just been saying .....

LINDA: I've been speaking metaphorically. We couldn't really get along.
It, would be like mixing matter with anti-matter.
Do you know that theory?

JOYCE: *(Shakes her head. A little miffed.)* No.

LINDA: There'd be an explosion. That's what would happen.
Oh, we'd get along for a while all right.
That's because our particular differences have a unique appeal for
each of us. But in the end we'd always ... blow up.

JOYCE: *(Suspicious.)* Are you playing games with me?

LINDA: What? Why would you think that?

JOYCE: You twist me one way, making me believe you want to be friends,
then you pull away, saying we can't.

LINDA: But we couldn't. I just explained .....

JOYCE: Forget it! I don't need to hear anymore **logical** explanations.
You're just a cold fish. A cold, intellectual fish.
Not a person with true feelings at all.
I ought to make you muck out my stall.

LINDA: Muck out your stall?

JOYCE: You heard me. *(Turns away.)* I'm going now.

LINDA:	What do you mean? Going where?
JOYCE:	Out of my room so I won't have to look at me ..... you .... the mirror! *(With disgust.)* Treating me like an experiment.
LINDA:	Wait! Wait! Don't go. You're right. I've treated you ... both of us ... like an experiment. Maybe that's one big way I'm opposite, in a bad way, from you. *(Pause.)* I'm sorry.
JOYCE:	*(Comes back.)* No more analysis?
LINDA:	I promise.
JOYCE:	*(Considers.)* Well. okay. *(Impulsively.)* Shake.

(They try to shake hands but the mirror prevents them.)

LINDA:	Um ... let.'s just wave at each other.

(They wave.)

JOYCE:	I wonder when we'll get our mirrors back.
LINDA:	I don' t know. You know, this could be permanent.
JOYCE:	Permanent? Now wait a minute. I like a little privacy in my bedroom. Not that I have weird habits, you understand. It's just that I'm not an exhibitionist.
LINDA:	*(Doesn't hear. Wanders from mirror.)* That would offer a lot of possibilities. A long range study of opposites.
JOYCE:	*(Warningly.)* There you go again. *(Pause.)* Hey, you're getting fuzzy.
LINDA:	We could see how we grow up and change. See each other as teenagers, adults, wives. Or I guess in your case, not a wife but a ..... **handsome matron.**

JOYCE: Listen! Listen to me! You're fading away.
                And I can hardly hear you.

LINDA: Me, as a successful scientist. You, as a famous equine gormet
                and showjumper.

JOYCE: Hello?! Hello?! She's gone.

LINDA: *(Turns to mirror. Face falls.)* She's gone.

                *(*LINDA *and* JOYCE *approach the mirror.*
                Slowly they raise their right hands. Wave.)

LINDA:}
JOYCE:}   Bye.

THE 23RD FLIGHT

Cast:	2 female
Playing time:	10 minutes
Costumes:	Contemporary dress
Properties:	Two chairs/seats
Setting:	Inside a passenger jet
Lighting:	No special effects
Characters:	Barb
	Tina

BARB and TINA are seated next to one another.

TINA: Well, that's that.

BARB: *(Opens eyes. Tense.)*   We're up?

TINA: Into the blue. Nice day, hmm?

BARB: *(Ignores question.)*   Have you flown before?

TINA: This will be my twenty-third time. I love it.

BARB: *(Not in agreement.)*   Uh-hunh.

TINA: And you? What about you?

BARB: *(Shrugs.)*   I don't know.
            Hundreds .... Several hundred.

TINA: Really? What are you in sales or something?

BARB: *(Still somewhat anxious.)* No. I'm an inspector.

TINA: Oh! You have to go to a lot of different places and inspect things?
              (BARB nods.) And they pay you to fly all over?
              Wow! Nice job.

BARB: *(Unenthusiastic.)* Nice.

TINA: I fly purely for pleasure. When I can afford it, of course.
              My uncle can get discounts, but only for his immediate family
              - **unfortunately** for me.
              None of them likes to fly.
              A shame. What I would do if I could get tickets cheap!

BARB: Your uncle works for the airlines?

TINA: *(With pride.)* Well, sort of. He **designs** them.

BARB: *(Perks up.)* Really? He must be quite an engineer.

TINA: *(Correcting.)* **Aerodynamical** engineer.
              He never really has to go to the factory and get his hands dirty
              putting them together. He's in the upper ranks.

BARB: So he's never really been involved with the construction.
              Has he even flown on one?

TINA: Sure has. *(Thinks.)* He must have.
              (Pause.) Actually, I've never heard of him flying.
              Isn't that funny?

BARB: *(Pointedly.)* So you have an uncle who designs planes
              he never builds, never flies on, never **sees.**

TINA: Well, it doesn't matter that much anyway, does it?
              I mean, designs can be tested on computers.
              Then the construction people simply take the blueprints
              and follow instructions. Like putting together a Christmas toy.

BARB: Remember those toys you couldn't put together correctly?

TINA: *(Frowns.)*   Well, perhaps I picked a poor analogy.

BARB: I think it's a good one.
                 If you don't follow a product from beginning to end
                 how do you know it's perfected?
                 Or even safe?
                 The upper ranks **need** to get their hands dirty.
                 That's the only way they can be sure their plans are being followed.

TINA: *(Indignant.)* But they hire specialists.

BARB: Specialists can only work with what they're given.
                 They don't make changes.
                 If there's a mistake, they can't spot it the way your uncle can.
                 They're merely following orders.

TINA: Well, airplanes are different.
                 People are more careful when they make them.

BARB: Airplanes are not different.

TINA: Well! How do you know?

BARB: *(Anxious again.)*   Because they are what I inspect.

TINA: Oh! Well, you could have told me before.
                 It wasn't very nice of you to make me feel foolish.

BARB: I apologize. I should have.
                 It's just that I'm a little upset.

TINA: *(Forgiving.)*   Oh! That's all right.
                 (Compassionate.) Can I help?

BARB: *(Shakes her head.)* No.

TINA: But I'm sure it would help to talk about it.

BARB: *(Smiles condescendingly.)*   I really, really don't think so.

TINA: *(Offended.)* Well! I don't know how you can be so certain.

BARB: Well ... because ... I inspected your uncle's planes.

TINA: Oh! *(Pause.)* There's something wrong with them?

BARB: *(Pointedly.)* There's something wrong with all of them.

TINA: Oh! *(Pause.)* Nothing serious?

BARB: Yes. I'm afraid so.

TINA: **All** of them?
             (BARB nods.) Wow. Uncle Bill never mentioned anything about it.

BARB: He doesn't know yet. I've just completed a nationwide inspection
             in order to confirm our suspicions.

TINA: Oh, no. Poor Uncle Bill. It'll kill him.

BARB: Unfortunately he won't be the only one.

TINA: I beg your pardon?

BARB: We're **on** one of Uncle Bill's planes.

TINA: Oh. *(Alarmed.)* **Oh!**

BARB: (Nods.) 'Oh', is right.

TINA: But ... there must be hundreds of planes.
             You didn't necessarily inspect this particular one.
             This one just might be safe.

BARB: They were all built the same way.
             They all have the same flaw.

TINA: So why did you get on one?

BARB: *(Waves hands in air.)* A mistake.
             I didn't realize what model plane this was until we were
             taxiing down the runway. I've had a lot on my mind lately.

TINA: Well, then, we have to turn the plane around.
             Isn't it that simple? Why aren't you up there now talking to the pilot?

BARB: *(Shrugs.)* I could be halfway up the aisle when the plane
             decides to take a nose dive.

TINA: But it might not!

BARB: It might not. We might make it all the way to the next airport.

TINA: And you don't care either way?
           We could get killed or not and you don't care?

BARB: *(Confidentially.)* Well, my life hasn't been that great.
           No excitement. Maybe it's best this way.

TINA: What are you saying? I like life.
           In fact, I believe living is one of my most favorite things to do.
           Won't you speak to the pilot just for me?

BARB: It really won't do any good.
           Even if I tell him he'll have to communicate with his boss.
           Then his boss will have to contact my boss.
           Even with an emergency finding like mine it could take hours
           before they decide whether to make us go back or proceed.
           By then, we'll either be at our destination collecting our luggage
           (Pause.) or we'll be ....

TINA: So it's hopeless?

BARB: You could go up there.

TINA: Me? They wouldn't believe me.

BARB: You never know. Tell them who your uncle is. *(Smiles.)*

TINA: This is starting to become funny to you, isn't it?
           Should I put on a silly hat and do a little dance?

BARB: That might be a nice way to go. Can you sing as well?

TINA: *(Starts to get angry then quiets down.)* I'll give you money.
           All you want. I'll write you a check right now.

BARB: Where would I spend it?
           I don't think Heaven has full service banks.

TINA: But we might **not** crash. Not if you do something.

BARB: Can we talk about something else?
I think we've worn this topic out.
I wonder if they serve food on this flight?
That was the one thing I disovered when I did my inspections:
this airline has great food. The smoked salmon especially.

TINA: *(Starts to get suspicious.)* How can you talk about food?
My stomach is twisted up around my heart and you're
talking about food? *(Decides to try something.)* Well,
I guess there's nothing to do but wait. *(Looks around.)*
On the other hand, why wait? Why prolong the agony?

BARB: What? What did you say?

TINA: I said, we might as well not wait around for it to happen.

BARB: We have no choice. What are you talking about?

TINA: *(Points to window of plane.)* See that? Emergency exit.
All I have to do is pull the red lever and it will open.

BARB: *(Laughs.)* But we'd be sucked out.

TINA: Exactly. *(Reaches over.)*

BARB: *(Shocked. Grabs TINA's arm.)* What are you doing?
TINA: Letting my uncle off the hook. At, least this time.

BARB: We'd be killed!

TINA: What are you getting so upset for?

BARB: You must be crazy.

TINA: Hunh? What have I been listening to these last few minutes
but your cheerful willingness to end it all?

BARB: But, well ... yes ... but, what you're doing is so immediate ......
so certain.

TINA: I see. You're a gambler.
You're gambling that the plane won't crash.
And you're betting your life, mine, everyone else's is that it?

BARB: (Looks away.) Um, sort of.

TINA: And what exactly are the odds of the plane going down?

BARB: There's ... um, a five percent chance we'll crash.
There's a time factor involved and, uh, most of your uncle's planes
haven't been flying long enough for stress to ... to work on the affected part.

TINA: *(Condescendingly.)* So you just wanted to scare me.
I can't believe it! I feel very sorry for you.

BARB: *(Remorseful.)* I'm sorry. I didn't mean to frighten you.
I suppose I'm not a very good person. I guess I really wouldn't mind
if that ten percent chance caught up with me.

TINA: You said **five** percent.

BARB: Uhh, exactly.

TINA: *(Even more suspicious.)* Is there really anything wrong with these planes?

BARB: *(Keeps face averted.)* Um. No.

TINA: Do you even inspect planes?

BARB: *No.*

TINA: *(Disbelief.)* Do you inspect **anything**?

BARB: Oh yes. Door hinges.

TINA: *(Mouth falls open.)* Door hinges.

BARB: Yes. Those things attached to your ....

'TINA: *(Interrupts.)* I know what they are.
You are unbelievable.

BARB: I know. Maybe you **should** pull that red handle.
It's what I deserve. I'm so ashamed.
But you see my job is pretty dull,
so I sometimes make up these things.
I even lied about the number of times I've flown.
This is really my first. I'm terribly sorry.

TINA:	And you should be. You're lucky, I don't intend to report you to the Door Hinge Association.
BARB:	There's no such thing.
TINA:	Well. Report you to somebody.
BARB:	I understand.
TINA:	You're awful.
BARB:	*(Contrite.)* I am.
TINA:	A horrible liar.
BARB:	True.
TINA:	I don't know that I'll speak to you the rest of the trip.
BARB:	I don't blame you. *(Hesitantly.)* Are you going to tell your Uncle Bill? He might cause a lot of trouble for me.
TINA:	No.
BARB:	*(Relieved.)* Oh, thank you. I'm very grateful.
TINA:	*(Pause.)* Mainly because I don't really have an Uncle Bill. *(BARB startled, looks at her. TINA smiles.)*

THE SHIRT IN QUESTION

Cast:	2 female
Playing Time:	10 minutes
Costumes:	Contemporary dress (RITA might be better dressed than RUTH)
Properties:	Table, SALE sign, white shirt, other clothing, paper money, a can
Setting:	A department store
Lighting:	No special effects
Characters:	Ruth
	Rita

RUTH and RITA approach a sale table heaped with clothes
from opposite sides without noticing each other.

RUTH: *(Rummaging.)* There must be one .... **ONE.**

RITA: *(Picking up clothes and flinging them down.)* No. No. No. No. No.

RUTH: *(Discovers a white sleeve. Looks at cuff.)* Can it be?

RITA: *(Discovers other sleeve.)* Aha! *(Each pulls up sleeve. Shirt clears pile.*
           They have same shirt.)

RUTH: Uh-oh.

RITA: Ee-yeah.

RUTH: Look. We can argue about who picked up the first sleeve .....
           or you could just give it to me, now.

RITA:	*(Smiles menacingly.)* Oh? And do you have a good doctor?
RUTH:	You don't waste any time getting around to making threats, do you?
RITA:	I don't have time to waste.
RUTH:	*(Firmly.)* Neither do I.
RITA:	*(Tries a different approach.)* I'll give you ten dollars for this.
RUTH:	**What?** But all these items are on sale for one dollar
RITA:	That's right. But I have no time to look elsewhere. And it's the only white shirt on the table.
RUTH:	Well. **I** need a white shirt. And I'm down to my last dollar.
RITA:	Then take this ten, go to another store, and get one.
RUTH:	As I said, I don't have much time either. Please. This shirt is very important to me.
RITA:	Me as well. It's going to be a **wedding** present.
RUTH:	I need mine for a wedding, too, but not ...... *(Pause. Snidely.)* Kind of a weird cheap wedding gift, isn't it?
RITA:	But I have a reason. I don't **like** the person.
RUTH:	*(Sighs.)* Look, what do I have to do to convince you that my need takes precedence over yours?
RITA:	There's nothing you can do. This shirt will provide me with an opportunity that comes around only once in lifetime. I can't pass it up.
RUTH:	*(Resolute.)* I'm not going to let go of this shirt.
RITA:	Neither am I. *(They look silently at each other.* *They give little tugs on the sleeves.)* Look, I'll tell you a little story. Maybe that will convince you.

RUTH: A little story? A little **story**? You mean a little lie.

RITA: No. I swear. *(Tries to hold up right hand but it is holding the sleeve. Switches the sleeve to left hand and raises right .)*
I swear on this shirt that it's the truth.

RUTH: Okay. I'm listening.

RITA: A few years ago my father lost his job.
He was approached by a man with a business proposition.
And this man made certain ..... promises ....

RUTH: *(Interrupts.)* Wait a minute.
Is this supposed to break my heart?

RITA: Just ... just wait till you hear it all.
Now ... he promised Pa would make a lot of money
in a real estate venture.
He just needed some capital to invest, and they'd be set.
Well, Pa checked it out. It all seemed legal and proper.
But he fooled Pa. He fooled everybody involved.

RUTH: And your family lost everything, right ?

RITA: On the contrary.
He was arrested, jailed and Pa got his money back .

RUTH: I don't get it.

RITA: I carry grudges. A long time.

RITA: I see. So you're sending him a cheap shirt on his wedding day?
Doesn't sound like much of a way of getting even.

RITA: *(Smiles.)* There's more to it than that.

RUTH: Oh?

RITA: Yes .... But I've given you my reason. What about yours?

RUTH: Mine's simple. The groom needs a white shirt.
He tore the one he had when he got out of the car at the church.
Of course he doesn't have a spare with him. *(Checks watch.)*
I have fifteen minutes to get across town.

RUTH: I didn't realize till I got here that I only have a dollar.
And I don't have time to go out and spend **your** ten.
Now please ....

RITA: But there are no ruffles down the front of the shirt.

RUTH: But it doesn't need ruffles.

RITA: He **must** have a ruffled shirt to go with his tuxedo.

RUTH: He's not wearing a tuxedo.

RITA: No tuxedo? A plain white shirt? Sounds like a terribly drab affair.

RUTH: *(Sarcastic.)* The President and First Lady couldn't make it,
so the ceremony was toned down.

RITA: Plain punch at the reception, I'll bet.
How boring.

RUTH: *(Defensive.)* That's right. No champagne. No caviar.
No butlers to tuck napkins in the guests' collars
and stick grapes in their mouths.

RITA: Sounds **horrible**.
Just like the one I'm going to attend.

RUTH: Really? But you're going to **lower** yourself to go anyway?

RITA: Yes.
I'll go to any lengths to have my fun.
Tell me, who is the unfortunate bride?

RUTH: *(Bristles.)* My sister.

RITA: Oh. *(Insincerely.)* I guess I've been hitting below the belt.
I'm terribly sorry.

RUTH: I'll accept your apology by relieving you of this shirt.

RITA: Oh no you won't.

RUTH: But you must see how much more urgent my need is.
There'll be a bare-chested groom going up the aisle!

RITA: If you haven't noticed by now ... I'm a very selfish person.
          The wedding I'm attending is beginning shortly too;
          and I must get my gift in with the rest.
          I wouldnt want to be spotted.

RUTH: What do you mean?

RITA: I want to slip my gift in anonymously, you see.
          I'm afraid the groom will burn the shirt if he knows who it is from.

RUTH: That makes sense.

RITA: Good.

RUTH: But I'm not turning loose the shirt.

RITA: Maybe ..... maybe if I let you in on the details of my plan
          you'll change your mind.
          Once you see how sneaky it is, how perfect my revenge will be,
          you'll see the light.

RUTH: I doubt it.

RITA: Well, anyway.
          Here's my secret ingredient: itching powder.
          *(RITA reaches into a pocket and pulls out a small can
          to show RUTH.)*

RUTH: **What?**

RITA: Itching powder! Isn't the idea terrific?
          I'll sprinkle itching powder in the shirt before I deliver it.

RUTH: *(Bored.)* Wow.
          (Yawns.) That's really getting him good, all right. Gee.

RITA: Not too excited, hunh? *(RITA replaces can in her pocket.)*
          Let me explain a bit more.
          I'm including a note. Without mentioning my name
          I'll say I'm an old, old friend,
          and that it would doing me a big favour to wear the shirt
          within the next few days.

35

RUTH: So what?
As soon as he puts it on he'll realize what's wrong and take it off.
He'll forget the whole thing in a minute,
figuring it to be a late bachelor party joke.

RITA: Ah, but that won't be the end of it.
He may take off the shirt, but the powder will stay.
Guaranteed! The stuff works into the skin and doesn't come out
with any amount of washing or scrubbing.
He'll be miserable for days! The honeymoon will be ruined.
Isn't it a diabolical idea?

RUTH: Don't you know you're acting like a child?

RITA: *(Unconcerned.)* Of course. There's no other excuse for me.
And Wesley, being a child in his own right, is the perfect recipient.

RUTH: Who?

RITA: Wesley. The groom.

RUTH: Wesley? What's his last name?

RITA: Hammond.

RUTH: *(Stunned.)* Oh, no! Oh! It can't be.

RITA: What? What is it? Are you having some sort of a fit?

RUTH: Wesley Hammond. My sister is marrying him.

RITA: *(Long pause. She bursts into laughter.)* Unbelievable!
Oh, this is too much. The irony of it all.
Just the sort of thing you'd find in a play.

RUTH: *(Upset.)* Well, this is no play. This is real.
And my sister is marrying Wesley Hammond, a criminal,
a man convicted of fraud.

RITA: Oh, that was just the last time.

RUTH: *(Gasps.)* **What?**

RITA: Listen. Wesley has been involved in all sorts of scandals.
           Fraud is just one of his many ways for getting around the world.

RUTH: *(Closes her eyes.)* Don't tell me.

RITA: He's bribed, blackmailed, bootlegged his way into the bank books of many.

RUTH: What will I do? My poor sister.

RITA: Well, obviously you'll have to get over to the church
           and put an end to things.
           Wesley is not the type to stay married for very long.

RUTH: But what could he be after? She's not rich.

RITA: Who knows? She could be a small piece in a very large puzzle.
           Maybe in order for his latest scam to succeed he needs to look
           very respectable, settled.

RUTH: This is awful. But I'll never convince my sister he's no good.
           She's one of those incurable romantics, you know?
           Love at first sight and all that.

RITA: There must be someone you can talk to.

RUTH: *(Shakes head.)* No. Everybody **likes** him.

RITA: *(Rolls eyes.)* That's Wesley all right.

RUTH: What if I was to approach him?
           Tell him what I know?
           Won't that shake him up?

RITA: I'm afraid not.
           You're dealing with a man who has swindled millions.
           He has nerves of steel.
           No, your knowing will make no difference to him.

RUTH: Then, that's it. *(Hopelessly.)* There's nothing to be done.

RITA: There's one small consolation.
           I'm sure she won't have to put up with him for very long.
           And she'll still be young enough to make a future for herself
           after he's gone.

RUTH: But ..... if there was only **something** .... *(RUTH looks at shirt.)*
I can't believe I've been out trying to help him.
I **ought** to let him go up the aisle bare chested.
That would be better than having him pretend to be eternally
grateful to me as he ....
(Pause. RUTH slowly grins.) ..... as he
slips into the shirt, then **immediately**
goes to stand in front of **hundreds** of people.
(RUTH smiles, hands the shirt to RITA.
RITA understands, smiles back
and pats the pocket containing the can of itching powder.)

A ROBBER AND A THIEF

Cast:	1 male, 1 female
Playing Time:	10 minutes
Costumes:	Contemporary dress
Properties:	Smart bag/purse, water pistol, toy gun, comb, small mirror, rag, roll of paper money, aspirin bottle
Setting:	A park
Lighting:	Slow fade to black during ANN'S last line

Characters:	Tom
	Ann

TOM is pacing back and forth across the stage.

TOM: *(Stops and looks at audience.)* This is a waste of time.
(Looks around.) There's nobody going to come by here.
I knew that before I came. *(Looks around.)*
I can't find honest work and I'm too chicken to rob.
I **tell** myself I can, then I get a pistol go into town,
and find the remotest spot in the park to waste the night away.
I guess I can get by as I am for a while, but I can't spend
the rest of my life getting thrown out of
restaurants and hotels for not paying.
Ah, well. Just about quitting time.
(Looks at pistol.) Time for bed, Daisy.
(Squirts water. Looks at audience.) Some crook, couldn't hurt a fly.
(Noise off stage.)
Oh no! There's somebody coming. Must be my unlucky night.
Well, Daisy.
I hope they look at you and not at me, or they'll know I'm a fake.

(ANN enters. Doesn't see TOM.
TOM *steps forward as she comes near.*)

TOM: Uh ....

ANN: *(Gasps.)* Oh!

TOM: *(Quickly.)* Don't scream. This is a gun.

ANN: *(Backs away slightly.)* A gun.

TOM: A gun.

ANN: Are you going to shoo ... shoo ... ?

TOM: No, I'm not going to shoot you.

ANN: *(Gasps at the word 'shoot.' But she looks somewhat relieved.)*
              Thank goodness.
              There's so much of that going around these days.

TOM: Yeah, well, all I want is your money.

ANN: My money?

TOM: Yeah, you know. Money.
              Don't tell me you don't have any! This **has** been a bad night.

ANN: Well, I ....

TOM: Maybe you're holding out. *(Waves gun in front of her face.*
              ANN *follows it with her eyes.)* This is a gun.

ANN: I know. You told me.

TOM: Oh! So, anyway, if you don't give me your money
              I'll have to .... to .... you know, do what you said.

ANN: Shoot me?

TOM: Shoot you. *(ANN starts to faint.)* Hey, don't faint!
              Don't turn ghastly white. I hate ghastly white.
              It makes me nauseous.

ANN: *(Steadies herself.)* I'm sorry.

TOM: Look, it's late, I'm tired, Daisy's tired ....

ANN: Daisy?

TOM: *(Holds up gun.)* Daisy.
                  (Ominously.) She's had a long night, too.

ANN: Oh!

TOM: So come on. I want to get home to catch the last of the news.
                  They're interviewing Jimi Hendrix.

ANN: But he's dead.

TOM: It's a rebroadcast. Slow news day. Isn't video tape wonderful?

ANN: It has its moments.

TOM: I'd like to chat some more, but I really have to go.
                  Your money?

ANN: My money?

TOM: Why do you always echo me?

ANN: I'm sorry.

TOM: And stop saying you're sorry!

ANN: I'm sorry. *(Starts to sniff.)*

TOM: Hey! Please don't cry.
                  Hey! That makes me nauseous too. Women!

ANN: What kind of a crack is that?

TOM: Was what?

ANN: **'Women!'**

TOM: *(Looks her up and down.)* Well I don't **think** I've made a mistake.

ANN: That's not what I mean.
              You implied that only women, never men, break down and cry
              under sudden and extreme emotional stress.

TOM: I didn't.

ANN: You did.

TOM: Look, I don't want to argue with you. Give me your money.

ANN: *(Angry now.)* No.

TOM: Give me your money.

ANN: *(Defiantly.)* No.

TOM: Give me your money.

ANN: *(Courageously.)* **No!**

TOM: I'm getting a headache.

ANN: Was it something I said?

TOM: You're not behaving the way a victim should.
              I know. I've read all the right magazines.
              And they all say that a victim's best chance of surviving a robbery
              without injury is to cooperate.

ANN: I don't have much time to read.

TOM: Figures.

ANN: Mostly I read biographies on women.
              Famous women whose names have lived down through history.
              Who have been models for us all.
              (Takes list from purse and hands it to TOM.*)*

TOM: *(Startled.)* These women killed people.

ANN: I know. Don't you get a sense of strength just seeing their names?

TOM: No. They just make my head hurt more.

ANN: Would you like an aspirin?

TOM: You got one?

ANN: Sure, hold on. *(Rummages through purse. Pulls out mirror.)*
Hold this, please. *(Gives him mirror. Rummages. Pulls out comb.)*
And this. *(Gives him comb. Rummages.*
Pulls out large roll of paper money.) And this.
(Gives him money. Rummages.) Ahh!
(Pulls out aspirin bottle.) Okay. *(She holds out purse to him*
and TOM dumps everything back in.) Take one of these.
(Gives him an aspirin, puts bottle back in purse.)

TOM: Thanks .... uh ....

ANN: Ann.

TOM: Thanks, Ann. You don't happen to have a glass of water
in there, do you?

ANN: *(Checks purse.)* Nope.

TOM: Hmm. Oh well. *(Takes aspirin.)*
Now, Ann, I've really got to hold you up and get home.
(Pause.) What am 1 saying? I feel like I'm holding up a friend.
Why did you tell me your name? That's what did it.
Let's forget the whole thing. *(Turns to go.)*

ANN: Wait! *(TOM turns)* What's **your** name?

TOM: Tom.

ANN: Tom what?

TOM: Tom Ste ...... Oh, no you don't.
If you know my name you can get me arrested.

ANN: I wouldn't do that.

TOM: Sure.

ANN: I wouldn't. *(Shyly.)* You're cute.

TOM: Look, you don't have to rub it in.

ANN: Rub what in?

TOM: Come on. You're making fun of me
just because I can't pull off a stupid hold-up.

ANN: I'm not. We're not communicating very well here.
Can't you see by my face I'm sincere?

TOM: You have a little spaghetti sauce on the corner of your mouth.

ANN: Oh! *(Turns away and wipes it off.)*
Now who's making fun?

TOM: I was just stating a fact.

ANN: Boy, some romantic. Aren't there times when you just want
to sweep a girl off her feet?

TOM: Yes. *(Pause.)* Good night. *(Turns to go.)*

ANN: Wait! *(TOM sighs, turns around.)* You going steady?

TOM: No.

ANN: Dating?

TOM: Sometimes.

ANN: You ..... uh ..... live by yourself?

TOM: Just me and Daisy.

ANN: I live by myself ... too.

TOM: *(Uninterested.)* Oh.

ANN: It's not ..... far. *(TOM takes out rag.)* My apartment, that is.
Just a few blocks away. *(TOM starts polishing Daisy.)* It's **mine** ...
.... live by **myself**. *(TOM continues polishing. ANN grabs him
under the chin and turns his head around to face her.)* **Alone.**

TOM: *(Chin still crushed between her fingers. He squeaks out his words.)* I … really …. have …. to …. go.

ANN: *(Looks into his eyes.)* You like my eyes?

TOM: *(Long pause.)* Not particularly.

ANN: *(Releases him.)* Jerk.

TOM: I'm sorry. You're a nice girl and all, but ….. I'm going.

ANN: So this is it, huh?

TOM: Afraid so. Bye.

ANN: Bye. *(TOM turns to go.)* **Tom!**
(TOM stops but doesn't turn around, sighing again.
ANN pulls out a gun and points it at him. Menacingly.)
Drop the gun.

TOM: What? *(Turns around shocked. Drops rag. Offers her the pistol.)*
Ann?

ANN: Yes, Tom?

TOM: I like your eyes.

ANN: Too late, Tom. Give me your money.

TOM: I don't **have** any money. That's why I'm out here.

ANN: You said Daisy was busy all night.

TOM: I lied.

ANN: Guess I'll have to shoot you, then.

TOM: Shoot me?

ANN: Don't echo me, Tom.

TOM: This is no line of work for you, Ann. You might get hurt.

ANN: I don't seem to be having any trouble right now.

TOM: That's because you don't see the hidden dangers.

ANN: Such as?

TOM: Well ... you might break a nail pulling the trigger.

ANN: Really, Tom, you're doing a lousy job of trying to help your case.

TOM: Well, now, wait, just wait. Let's see. Ah! You might
have forgotten to load your gun with bullets.

ANN: I didn't forget.

TOM: You didn't? *(Squirts water pistol aimlessly.)* I did.

ANN: You walk around trying to rob people with **that**?
Tom, you are a real amateur.

TOM: I know. *(Drops the pistol)*
It was much easier stealing tips off tables in restaurants.

ANN: You're pathetic.

TOM: But I'm a harmless pathetic. Can't you appreciate that?
I mean, you were in absolutely no danger from me the entire time.

ANN: You still scared me out of ten years growth.

TOM: Who knows? They might have been lousy years anyway.
I know that **my** last ten years haven't been all that great.
Why, I remember one winter in particular ......

ANN: Tom.

TOM: Hunh?

ANN: Shut up.

TOM: Oh. I just thought I'd ....

ANN: Turn around. *(TOM turns around.)*
            I'm going to count to ten and then shoot you.

TOM: Why ten?

ANN: Nine, then.

TOM: Sorry I asked.

ANN: *(As she counts the lights dim to black.)* One ..... two .....
            three .... four .... five .... six .... seven .... eight .... nine.
            (Stage is black. Pause.) **Bang!**

DIARY

Cast:	2 female or 1 female and 1 male
Playing Time:	15 minutes
Costumes:	Contemporary dress, black unisex look diary
Properties:	Armchair, pencil
Setting:	Girl's bedroom.
Lighting:	No special effects

Characters: Diane
                Diary

DIARY is sitting in a chair, head bowed. DIANE enters
and 'opens' DIARY.

DIARY: Uh-Oh! Here we go again.
           Miss Fantasy is on the warpath.

DIANE: *(Pretends to write.)* Dear Diary .....

DIARY: **Ow!** What do you have to make your pencil so sharp for all the time? You're
           not pushing a pin into a pincushion; you're writing in your dear old Diary.

DIANE: Oops! *(Goes away to resharpen pencil.)*

DIARY: *(Horrified.)* Look what you've done! You've stabbed me!
           You've poked the tip of your lead through three whole pages and broken it off!
           Oh! The room is spinning. I feel like I've been run through with a saber.

DIANE: Now, let's try that again.

DIARY: Oh no you don't.
           Ever since I've been your diary you've caused nothing but problems.
           You don't take care of me, you don't let me associate with any of those
           handsome looking books over on your shelf, you just keep me
           locked away in your desk. Well, no more.
           I quit.

DIANE: What should I say first?

DIARY: I'm telling you, I quit.
           You just forget about scrawling another entry in me.

DIANE: *(Pretends to write.)* Tonight I had the most fantastic date
           of my entire life.

DIARY: I'm not listening.
           If you're going to be obnoxious and ignore me, well then
           I just don't care **what** you have to say.

DIANE: Brad was a perfect gentleman.

DIARY: *(Suddenly interested.)* Brad?
           You finally got a date with Brad ?

DIANE: First, we went to McDonald's.

DIARY: Yeah? Yeah? Don't stop now.
           (DIANE erases what she's written.) What are you doing?
           Oh no, not again. Not already. Not this early on.

DIANE: We went to a famous French restaurant.

DIARY: I can't believe it. You can't even **spell** restaurant.
           R-e-s-t-r-a-n-t. What is that?
           If you're going to lie at least make it look good.

DIANE: Our first course was ham-boo-gar au gratin.

DIARY: Who are you kidding?
           If a Frenchman reads this he'll pass out .

DIANE: To drink, we ordered their best bottle of Le Coke.

DIARY: Forget what I said. He wouldn't pass out.
            He'd shoot himself.

DIANE: Afterward we went to a movie. *(Erases.)*

DIARY: Oh no. Don't tell me you're going to put down the ballet again.

DIANE: We went to the ballet. The music and dance was spectacular.
            I especially liked the part where the hero danced on stage,
            threw a hand grenade at the bad guys and cut the ropes
            on the girl in distress using the knife he stole off that
            army guy riding the tank.

DIARY: What ballet was this? *(DIANE pauses to think.)*
            Diane, why can't you just be honest for once?
            There's nothing wrong with being an average teenager
            having a good time doing average things.
            Years from now, when you read these entries,
            you won't even recognize yourself.
            And you'll have forgotton what really happened and what it was like.
            Don't you think that will be sad?
            Don't you want to remember Brad the way he really was?
            For once in your life be honest with yourself.
            Come on. You can do it.

DIANE: After that. Brad had to beat up five guys who were teasing me.

DIARY: *(Rolls eyes.)* Oh, great.

DIANE: Fortunately Brad didn't hurt himself.
            In fact he was glad for the exercise,
            since it burned off some of that French dinner we had.

DIARY: I can't believe you're writing that down.
            Do you know that there are professional people who get paid
            about a hundred dollars an hour to help people like you?
            Where do you think your parents are going to get that kind of money?

DIANE: I like him a lot. But there seems to be something missing.

DIARY: Like what? A Rolls Royce?

DIANE: Anyway, after that he took me to the park to watch the submarine races.

DIARY: Submarine races? What are the submarine races?

DIANE: Submarine races are races that are held on the river
late at night by the naval base.
Only there really aren't any races.
It's just an excuse to go out to the park and ..... well, park.

DIARY: Oh, I get it. What will people think of next?
(DIANE goes off to think.) Well don't stop now!
You're getting to the good part!
That's the trouble with being a diary.
I'm nothing but a book with blank pages,
no memories, no plot, no thoughts at all
until somebody starts filling me up.
Why couldn't I have been born an adventure novel?
Then I'd already know how thing's were going to turn out in the end,
instead of waiting for Dumbo here to go on one of her rare dates.
Or make something up about her boring afternoons,
which is usually what happens.
I could have gone on to such great things as a novel.
I would have had more ambition for myself.
I could have tried to end up in somebody's nice study.
Or maybe a public library, standing up tall in a smart display rack.
Or, the highest honor, the Library of Congress!
Wouldn't that, have been something!
Instead I'm stuck here in some teenager's room filling up with stories
of childish romance.

DIANE: He said he loved me.

DIARY: See what I mean?

DIANE: He said he couldn't believe he'd lived this long without me.

DIARY: Enough, I think I'm getting sick.

DIANE: He thinks we should run off together like Romeo and Julict.

DIARY: Yeah. Sure.

DIANE: I just wish I didn't have to hurt my parents.

DIARY: Huh? Wait a minute. You're not serious are you?
           What about school?

DIANE: We can stow away aboard a freighter and go to New Zealand.
           They have lots of nice, fluffy sheep there.
           We can ranch and sell the wool.

DIARY: You are out of your wool gathering mind.
           It's cold in New Zealand. And I don't know anybody there.
           I'll never see my relatives again, my father the German dictionary,
           my mother the complete illustrated encyclopedia of snails.
           I'll even miss my brother who's sunk so low as to become
           a cheap comic strip paperback.
           Well. You just listen, Diane. Forget it.
           I'm not going anywhere, so you just better forget about leaving.

DIANE: I'll have to travel light. I won't be able to take much with me.
           Just the clothes on my back, I guess.

DIARY: *(Squeaks.)* What? You're leaving me?
           You can't do that! What will I do?
           Nobody wants a used diary.
           Oh, please take me with you. Please, please, please.

DIANE: I'll have to say goodbye to you, dear Diary.

DIARY: I'm doomed.

DIANE: I'll have to leave you here for my parents to find
           so they'll know what happened to me.

DIARY: Wonderful. They'll be so mad they'll use me to start a bonfire.

DIANE: Maybe by reading you they'll understand me better,
           and see why I'm doing this.

DIARY: I don't even understand why you're doing this.How will they?
           I'm sure they'll learn a lot about you when they read
           how you flew to Paris once, toured the museums, had lunch with a Count
           and got back here on the same day in time to go to choir practice.
           And what about that Saturday night they left you here alone?
           I'm sure they'll find it fascinating when they read
           how you defended the house against invaders from outer space
           by turning on the sprinkler and making them melt.

DIARY: *(DIANE makes a big X in* DIARY.*)* Hey! **Now** what are you doing?
                You crossed out the whole page.

DIANE: *(Sadly.)* Dear Diary, I'm sorry I've put down so many lies over the months.

DIARY: Huh?

DIANE: But I can't do it anymore because of tonight with Brad.

DIARY: This is a switch. You mean you're not going to New Zealand?
                I'm not going in the bonfire?
                What did you have to scare me like that for?

DIANE: I only wrote of those things because I was lonely.
                Yes, Diary, me, who's had all those big adventures.
                I had to make them up because my life as I've really been living it
                has been so boring.

DIARY: Well, now, I wouldn't say that.

DIANE: The only time I feel special, Diary, is when I'm with you.
                You don't make any demands on me.
                You don't tell me to clean my room, you don't think I'm dumb when I
                give wrong answers in class, and you let me go out with Prince Charming
                if you think that's what I need.

DIARY: I... Uh, well I, you know. I've always ... uh **tried** to do what's best for you.

DIANE: You don't care if I have fantasies. You let me live the life I've always
                wanted, right here in these very pages, until now.

DIARY: Look, uh ... some of those nasty things, I said before,
                like, uh, calling you Dumbo? Just, uh, just forget them, okay?

DIANE: You see. when I went out with Brad tonight, I realized that,
                no matter how great my fantasies, it's real life that I have to deal with first,
                and try to be happy in. Like I said about Brad. We went out tonight and all,
                but we didn't do anything special. And we didn't go to the park, either.
                He brought me home early. So early even I was embarrassed.
                I asked if he'd call me. He didn't answer.
                He pretended like he didn't. hear. He just drove off, left me standing there.

DIARY: If only I'd known how much you cared about me,
          I wouldn't have been so hard on you.
          I would have understood.
          If only you'd have let me listen to the real you.
          Gosh, you look terrible. Listen, I've got an idea!
          Why don't you forget about Brad and, just for tonight, pretend again.
          Yeah! Sure! Why don't you go to Paris again.
          Or maybe someplace new?
          London? Athens? Rome? Come on Diane, you can do it.
          (DIANE slowly raises pencil.)
          That's it. That's it. You can do it.

DIANE: *(Writes slowly.)* I'm tired, Diary, and I think I'll go to sleep.
          I promise to write only the truth, from now on.
          And if it's something sad, well, I guess pretending
          isn't going to make the sadness get any better.
          So, only the truth. Only the truth.
          (Puts down pencil. Walks slowly off stage.)

DIARY: Diane? Diane? Wait. You can't leave me like this.
          I feel bad now with this new stuff written in me.
          At least with the adventure stories I could get a good laugh.
          But this. This doesn't make me feel very good.
          I don't want to know about it. Diane? Diane?
          I didn't realize how nice a job I had listening to you before.
          Please. Come back and change this.
          Make it different.
          Diane? Diane? *(DIANE exits.)* I'm sorry. I'm sorry.

BUS STOP

Cast:	3 female
Playing time:	10 minutes
Costumes:	Contemporary dress
Properties:	Bus stop sign, large bag/purse, feather, jar with lid, towel, 3 eggs
Setting:	A suburban side walk bus stop
Lighting	No special effects
Sound:	An alarm clock bell

Characters: Jane
Paula
Mary

JANE and PAULA stand waiting for the bus.

JANE: *(Long pause before speaking.)* I am ..... a bird.

PAULA: *(Startled.)* **What?**

JANE: I am ..... *(Turns to* PAULA*.)* ..... a bird.

PAULA: Well! I don't think they allow animals on the bus. *(Laughs.)*

JANE: *(Not amused.)* Some might find that statement offensive.

PAULA: Listen! I didn't start this.

JANE: I am what I am ....

55

PAULA: *(Singing.)* ... 'and that's all that I am,
I'm Popeye the sailor man.'

JANE: There are **certain organizations** designed to take care
of people like you

PAULA: And there are rooms with padded walls designed for people like you.

JANE: I told you: I am not a people. I'm a bird.

PAULA: Okay. Okay. Can't we just wait quietly for the bus?
(Pause.) I think the driver must be a snail.
(Laughs sarcastically.)

JANE: Why is it so hard to believe?
You're **so** typical of the common populace.
You rely on empirical evidence ..... you can't take a straightforward
statement as the truth without proof.

PAULA: Okay. You're right.
I don't believe you're a bird
because you don't look like one.
And I won't believe it until you sprout feathers and ......
and eat a worm.

JANE: I do have feathers.

PAULA: *(Examines* JANE *with a hard look.)* **Oh?**

JANE: Yes. They're just covered up.
There's no reason to make a spectacle of myself
when I'm not flying.

PAULA: *(Rolls her eyes.)* **Flying!**

JANE: Yes. *(Reaches up her sleeve, yanks, winces, hands a feather to* PAULA.*)*
I hate to do that. Throws me off balance, aerodynamically speaking.
But since you require proof .....

PAULA: *(Stares at feather.)* You've totally lost all sense of reality, haven't you?

JANE: I beg your pardon?

PAULA: You know. Your brain. It's addled, turned to rancid margarine.

56

JANE: *(Sneers.)* I see. Even when confronted with
irrefutable evidence ……….

PAULA: *(Splutters.)* **Irrefutable?**

JANE: *(Ignors* PAULA.*)* As far as worms go …. I'm not hungry.

PAULA: What ? What about worms?

JANE.   You asked about them.

PAULA: Oh? Oh, yes. So I did.

JANE: *(Reaching into her bag.)* I do keep a snack on hand, though,
just in case. *(Takes off lid and extends jar toward* PAULA.*)*
Have one?

PAULA: *(Smiling.)* You expect me to believe you keep worms in that?
(Looks in jar. Gasps. Clutches her stomach.)
Good heavens!

JANE: *(Replaces jar.)* I'm really going out of my way with you
and I don't know why. Maybe it's because I've always wanted to
convince at least one of you.
But I see I've failed yet again.

PAULA: *(Stares at* JANE.*)* I think I'd better get help.

JANE: No, no. I'm afraid it's no use.
There's nothing either of us can do to help convince you.

PAULA: *(Starts to back away.)* I'll just go get.....

JANE: *(Shouts.)* **Watch it!**

PAULA: *(Jumps back towards* JANE *and turns around.)* **What?!**

JANE: *(Angrily.)* You almost stepped on that pigeon.

PAULA: *(Also angry.)* I've had about enough ….
(She is cut short by an alarm clock that goes off in JANE*'s bag.)*
Um … er, your bag is ringing.

JANE: *(Puts down the bag and takes out a small towel)*
Time to turn the little dears.
Could you hold out your hands?
(PAULA is too intrigued to refuse. Holds out hands.
JANE puts towel in PAULA's hands, unwraps it.
Three eggs sit in towel. JANE starts to turn them.)
I turn them regularly so they don't get cold on one side.
I have a hot water bottle in the bottom.

PAULA: You're kidding.

JANE: *(Impatient.)* Well! I can't sit on them all the time.

PAULA: I don't believe this.

JANE: Still skeptical. *(Lifts towel out of PAULA's hands.)*

PAULA: Skep ...? *(Gets an idea. Grabs an egg.)*

JANE: *(Anxiously.)* What are you doing?!

PAULA: I'm going to take this egg: which is obviously a chicken egg .....
and **splatter** it against the wall.

JANE: *(Horrified.)* You can't be serious.
(PAULA raises her arm to throw.) **My baby!**
My baby! **Please!** I'll do anything you say. Anything !
Just spare the dear yolk of my heart.

PAULA: Oh? Anything?

JANE: Yes! Yes!

PAULA: Deny it.

JANE: Deny what?

PAULA: That you're a bird, of course.

JANE: In all fairness to you I should warn that I'll even lie to
regain my child.

PAULA: I don't care.
All I want is to hear the words out of your mouth.

(JANE looks above PAULA's head. She relaxes.)

PAULA: So what are you so self-satisfied about, all of a sudden?

JANE: *(Nods toward the sky.)* Everything's all right, now; help's on the way.

PAULA: *(Wants to look up but doesn't.)* What? *(Thinks. Smiles.)*
Oh! I get it. You're going to tell me that a flock of your friends is
swooping down out of the sky to help you.
That it?

JANE: No.
There's just one coming.

PAULA: *(Pleased with herself for guessing right.)* Well!
I hope it's not that pigeon I almost stepped on or you're in trouble.
(Laughing.) His few ounces aren't going to be much of a match for me.

JANE: Oh, it's not the pigeon. *(Pause.)* It's my husband.

PAULA: *(Gasps.)* **What?!** *(Turns her head to look.)*

JANE: *(Snatches back egg while PAULA's attention is elsewhere.)* **Baby!**
(PAULA turns her back to JANE.) I told you I'd even lie.
(Puts egg back into her bag.)
You are an unwell person

PAULA: *(Sighs.)* Of course.
(MARY enters to wait for the same bus.)

JANE: *(To herself.)* Imagine! Threatening to kill my child.
(Startled. MARY begins to unobtrusively listen.)
(JANE sobbing quietly.) My goodness!
(Distraught.) Wanting to smash him against the wall!

MARY: *(Nudges JANE, indicates PAULA.)* Say, is this person bothering you?

PAULA: It's the other way around.

MARY: *(To PAULA.)* That's not the way I've been hearing it.

PAULA: *(Points to JANE.)* This ... 'lady' ....

JANE: *(Interrupts.)* This lady tried to commit murder.

59

PAULA: *(Laughs.)* Okay. Ask her where the child is.

MARY: *(Wary.)* Where's your child?

JANE: *(Indicates bag)* In there.

MARY: *(Stares at* PAULA, *shocked.)* What did you do to him?!

PAULA: *(Shouts)* It's an egg! **A stupid egg!**

MARY: That's not a good sign. *(To* JANE.*)* She's raving.
(Starts to back up and takes JANE *with her by the arm)*
I think we've got a dangerous case on our hands.

JANE: *(Stops* MARY.*)* *No,* no, no.
(Showing MARY *the bag.)* She means in here.

MARY: *(Looks inside. Perplexed.)* It's an egg. *(Pause.)*
It's several eggs. *(Pause.)* There are eggs in your bag.
(Pause.) Why are there eggs in your bag?

PAULA: *(Happy to explain.)* Don't you see? This 'lady' is a bird. See?
She even plucked one of her feathers to show me ...
And in her bag she keeps her 'unhatched children'...
Uh! Well, eggs!

MARY: *(Pause.)* ...... don' t get it.

PAULA: It's simple. This .... 'lady' ... is ... a bird.
You know. Tweet tweet! Eats **worms!!**

MARY: Eats worms?

JANE.   *(Offering.)* Have some?

PAULA: A one hundred percent, dyed in the wool, flies south for the winter, type bird.

MARY: *(Slowly.)* I see.

JANE: *(Beaming.)* **Well!** I'm glad we finally got it all straightened out.
(Looks at her watch.) I'm afraid I won't be able to wait any longer
for the bus. I'll have to resort to the more faithful way. *(JANE exits.)*

MARY: *(To* PAULA.*)* You didn't really believe she was a...a ... ?

PAULA: *(Shakes her head.)* No.
                       (They start laughing uproariously together.)

MARY: **Oh my!**
                       How long did you have to stand here and listen to her?

PAULA: I don't know but it seemed like forever.
                       (They attempt to compose themselves.)

MARY: A bird. Wow! *(She looks looks after* JANE.*)*
                       I wonder where she went?

PAULA: Probably grabbed a taxi. She said she was,
                       '... going to go the old faithful way.'

MARY: Yeah.
                       (Pause. They are facing the audience, waiting.
                       Gradually they lose their smiles.
                       After a few moments they raise their heads together
                       to look up at the sky.)

THE CLOCK WATCHERS

Cast:	4 male
Playing time:	15 minutes
Costumes:	Contemporary dress
Properties:	3 watches, I.0.U.s
Setting:	A town sidewalk
Lighting:	No special effects

Characters: Sam
Tom
Frown
Poor

(Tom, Frown and Poor may be played by the same person
if desired with simple change of props, such as hat, scarf, etc.,)

SAM is on the sidewalk engaged in conversation with TOM.

SAM: I don't understand.

TOM: You won the final hand last night, and now I'm paving off my I.0.U.

SAM: **That** I understand. You said you'd give me a watch.

TOM: And here it is.

SAM: But, it's got **two** faces.

TOM: Pretty nice, huh?

SAM: But why does it have two?

TOM: One was for the week, set ahead so I wouldn't be late for work.
      The other was set back, for weekends,
      so I'd take things slow and easy.

SAM: So which is which? They both look way off to me.

TOM: *(Frowns)* I'm not sure. I kept mixing them up and changing them.
      (Looks at another watch of his.) Well, I'm late for an appointment.
      See you. (TOM exits.)

SAM: Wait! So am I! What time is it? *(Looks in frustration at watch.*
      Enter. FROWN. SAM sees him, brightens.) Excuse me.
      Have you the time?

FROWN: The question should be, do I have the time to give you the time?
      That, is to say, do I have the time to spare?
      You see, time is a commodity. Almost as valuable as money.
      No, more valuable. What would be the use of money if we didn't
      have the time to make it?

SAM: All I want is the correct time.

FROWN: As one would want correct change for a dollar.
      But can I give you **my** minutes? Do you think they lie loose, jangling
      in my pocket? And just what could I exchange them for anyway?
      It's just not possible for me to give you sixty minutes for your one hour.
      It's just not possible. Einstein proved that, I think.
      Anyway .... *(Notices SAM's watch.)* My goodness.
      Does that watch have two faces?

SAM: Yes it does.

FROWN: *(Indignant.)* Well! I don't think that's fair.
      Why you have more time than me? I'm a hard working man.
      I pay my taxes. It's hard enough for me to get by
      with the mere twenty-four hours I've got.
      Why should you get any more?

SAM: It's just a watch.

FROWN: Don't give me that. I can see what you're up to.
      You've got twice as much time as the rest of us.

FROWN: *(Grabs* SAM*'s wrist.)*
Aha! See that? They don't even match!
Why, you could be at home asleep at five a.m.
and out having steak at seven p.m. at the same time.
It's just not fair!

SAM: *(Has an idea.)* tell you what.
Since you're obviously more deserving, I'll sell it to you.

FROWN: And wheedle what preposterous amount out of me?

SAM: I'll **give** it to you, if only you'll tell me the right time.

FROWN: *(Smiles.)* You are a shrewd bargainer.
Very well.
(Takes SAM*'s watch.)* The time is **precisely** nine thirty-six p.m.

SAM: What? But it's morning!

FROWN: Ah, but you're on **my** time now.

SAM: What does that mean?

FROWN: Well, you see. I do my best work at night.
I was simply not born to be a morning person.
But everyone else in my company worked during daylight.
So an adjustment had to be made.

SAM: So you made the adjustment.

FROWN: Oh no. **They** made it.
All of the clocks in my office building read just the same as my watch.
They are on my time, too.

SAM: But that's ridiculous. *(Points.)* There's the sun over there in the east.

FROWN: But I am standing **here**.
And as I could not possibly be up and functioning before one p.m.,
you are mistaken.

SAM: Look. A watch is a mechanical instrument, artificial and governed by man.
But you can't change nature! It's outside our management.

FROWN: On the contrary. *(Points at his watch.)* I've managed it quite well.
And now with your watch I'll manage even better.
(Adjusts SAM's *watch on his wrist.)* Now if you'll excuse me.
I think I'll take my afternoon nap and my evening bath.
*(*FROWN *exits.)*

SAM: Now I don't even have a wrong watch. *(Enter* POOR.*)*
Have you got the time please?

POOR: I'm all out of time, buddy. I'm that destitute.

SAM: *(To himself.)* Oh, no.

POOR: I can't even afford the time to stand here talking.

SAM: Then how do you survive?

POOR: *(Confidentially.)* I steal time.

SAM: That doesn't make sense.

POOR: Sure does. A guy who steals a break on a job is stealing time
from his boss. A man who is on the go all day,
and who rarely goes home, steals time from his wife and kids.

SAM: So whose time are you stealing now?

POOR: Yours of course. I bet you have a meeting to get to.

SAM: That's right.

POOR: See? I'm stealing your time from that meeting.

SAM: So what happens when you're all alone?
When there's nobody around for miles?

POOR: I write an I.0.U.

SAM: What?

POOR: Sure. *(Reaches into his pocket.)* See these?
This one's for some time I spent at the beach. It was windy that day,
so nobody else came. This one? That's from last Thursday.
I didn't have time to wash the dishes but I did them anyway.

SAM: And who do you write these I.0.U.s to?

POOR: To myself.

SAM: Why don't you just tear them up then?

POOR: *(Pause.)* I don't have time. *(SAM groans.)*
And even if I did I'd just have to write another I.O.U.
Time is hard these days. Hard to come by, much less hard to spend.
Do you remember? You used to be able to spend all day
riding from New York to Washington, D.C.
But now trains are faster. They get you there in **no** time.
.... And museums ..... you used to be able to fritter away your time there,
but not any more. Not with crowds the way they are.
At a special exhibit they rush you right through.

SAM: But doesn't that **save** you time?

POOR: Are you kidding? I saved an hour yesterday.
From five-oh-three to six-oh-three. Now, what am I going to do
with **two** of those today?

SAM: I don't know. I just talked to a guy who thought he knew what to do
with an extra **day**.

POOR: *(Shakes his head.)* That's terrible. A person like that ought to be arrested.

SAM: For what?

POOR: *(Thoughtfully.)* Can you imagine cramming your days full of things to do?
Filling your hours? Stuffing your minutes? Why, you'd be so busy
you wouldn't have time to enjoy the things you were doing.
And you know what that means?
Murder.

SAM: Murder?

POOR: You're killing time.

SAM: Oh! no. *(Rolls eyes.)*

POOR: That's right. Bloating it. Over indulging it. Abusing it
until you don't even know if it's there.
And once you forget time, ... you've killed it.

SAM: But you can't be aware of time .... all the time.

POOR: Of course not. But you can at least show some appreciation
         for it once in a while. Use it wisely, and you'll be thankful it's there
         when you need it. Spend time making a spare house key
         for a friend to hold and you'll be glad you did
         when you lock yourself out - you'll still be able to get to the play at curtain
         or have the place straightened for company; or tune in the beginning
         of the Superbowl. It's all a matter of respect for something valuable.

SAM: Oh yeah? Well what about you?
         Stealing time. Shouldn 't you be arrested too?

POOR: I guess in a way I'm guilty too.
         But I'm not taking it just to waste it. I use it.
         Wouldn't you steal a little bread from a store if you were starving

SAM: *(Grudgingly.)* I suppose so. But I'd first try to find a job
         and make a living for myself.

POOR: Well, I've tried that.
         More than once. And you know what?
         It was awful. I never had enough to do.
         I always found time on my hands. And when I thought
         about all those people who didn't have any time at all...
         (Shakes head sadly.) Well, I must be going.
         I'm afraid I've used up all your time. *(POOR exits.)*

SAM: *(Awkwardly.)* Uh, don't worry about it.
         (Pauses.) I'm think I'm getting a headache over this.
         I've run into someone who has too much time, and one who hasn't enough.
         I think I've got just the exact amount.
         But I still, don't, have the **right** time.
         (Enter TOM.) Tom!

TOM: Tell you what. I'll give you cash instead.
         I just couldn't bear the idea of being without that watch.
         Can I buy it off you?

SAM: Uh, ... sorry, Tom. But, it's gone.
         I gave it to someone in exchange for the wrong time.

TOM: What?

SAM: Don't worry. I don't think I understand it either.
        Listen. Do You have the time?
        Not time to spare, but the hour.
        You know what I mean?

TOM: Sure, Sam, sure.

SAM: Not stolen time, or wasted time ...... just regular time.
        You know? The big hand is on something,
        and the little hand is on something else?
        (Puts hand to forehead.) Do I have a headache.

TOM: It's eight-oh-two. Exactly.

SAM: Really?

TOM: Yeah.

SAM: That sounds right.
        But ..... You wouldn't lie to me would you?
        I mean, even though the sun **is** in the east?

TOM: Huh?

SAM: It's hard to explain, Tom.
        Just ... just assure me that it's eight-oh-two.

TOM: It's eight-oh-two.

SAM: *(Shakes* TOM*'s hand.)* Thanks, Tom. Thanks a lot.
        I appreciate that. You've done wonders for me.

TOM: *(Anxious to escape.)* Uh ... yeah, Sam. Sure.
        Uh ... see you . *(*TOM *exits.)*

SAM: Well, that's that. *(Dusts himself off.)* Everything's straight.
        (Looks around.) The world is back on course. An even keel.
        (Takes a deep breath.) Yes. Well. *(Pauses. Frowns.)*
        So why do I feel as though I'm out of time?

ADDITIONAL TITLES AVAILABLE

SOLO SCENES SERIES

THE SIEVE and **CABBAGE** provide invaluable monologue material with a wide variety of theatrical applications and are valid for LAMDA Junior Acting examinations. These short original scenes are proving popular for use with speech and drama pupils in the 8-14 year age range and beyond

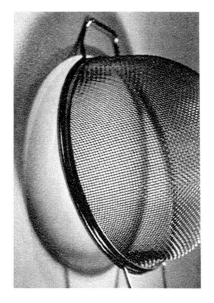

THE SIEVE AND OTHER SCENES
The first book
of original monologues
by Heather Stephens including
an adaptation of
THE LITTLE MATCH GIRL

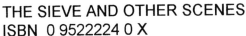

THE SIEVE AND OTHER SCENES
ISBN 0 9522224 0 X

CABBAGE AND OTHER SCENES
The second book
of original monologues
by Heather Stephens including
an adaptation of
THE PIED PIPER OF HAMELIN

CABBAGE AND OTHER SCENES
ISBN 0 9522224 5 0

*Dramatic Lines**

DUOLOGUES AND ONE ACT PLAYS

PEARS provides original acting material for two and includes adaptations of scenes from Aristophanes classic play Peace and Dickens Oliver Twist. The scenes are suitable for pupils in the 8-14 year age range and beyond

PEARS DUOLOGUES
The first book
of original scenes for two
by Heather Stephens

PEARS DUOLOGUES
ISBN 0 9522224 6 9

WILL SHAKESPEARE-SAVE US!
WILL SHAKESPEARE-SAVE THE KING!
Two one act plays by Paul Nimmo
in which famous speeches and scenes
from Shakespeare are acted out
as part of a comic story

WILL SHAKESPEARE-SAVE US!
WILL SHAKESPEARE-SAVE THE KING!
ISBN 0 9522224 1 8

WILL SHAKESPEARE is suitable for performance by a large or small cast aged 11 years upwards and equally suitable for theatre group performance to young people

a resource book by Antoinette Line 25 themed drama lessons suitable for junior and secondary pupils with lessons taught through improvisation using a selection of well known authors

DRAMA LESSONS IN ACTION

DR ... *ON*
DR ... *ON*
DR ... *ON*
DR ... *ON*
DR ... *ON*
DR ... *ON*
DR ... *ON*
DR ... *ON*
DR ... *ON*
DR ... *ON*
DR ... *ON*

DRAMA LESSONS IN ACTION

DRAMA IN ACTION
ISBN 0 9522224 2 6